This P.B. Bear book belongs to

. . . .

. . . .

P. B. Bear

Franny

Dermott

bed

pajamas

pants

shirt

door

snowballs

snow bear

pebbles

Christmas tree

beads

decorations

reindeer

sleigh

houses

presents

Mailman Monkey

Grandma Bear

Snow Bear

friends

package

invitation

Dear Mailman,
You are invited to my house for Christmas Day.
Love from P.B. Bear

sweater

hat

scarf

twigs

mugs

Christmas cards

fireplace

packages

books

star

window

stars

moon

presents

bowl

necklace

socks

stars

A DK PUBLISHING BOOK

Senior Designer Claire Jones
Designer Lisa Hollis
Editor Fiona Munro
Managing Art Editor Chris Fraser
Senior Editor Caryn Jenner
DTP Designer Kim Browne
US Editor Kristin Ward

Photography Dave King
Illustration Judith Moffatt
Production Katy Holmes

First American Edition, 1997
2 4 6 8 10 9 7 5 3 1

Published in the United States by DK Publishing, Inc.
95 Madison Avenue, New York, New York 10016
Visit us on the World Wide Web at http://www.dk.com

A catalog record for this book is
available from the Library of Congress.

ISBN 0-7894-2175-5

Color reproduction by Colourscan
Printed and bound in Italy by L.E.G.O.

Acknowledgments
DK would like to thank the following manufacturers
for permission to photograph copyright material:
Ty Inc. for "Toffee" the dog and "Freddie" the frog.
Merrythought Ltd. for the monkey.

DK would also like to thank the following people
for their help in producing this book:
Patricia Tregunno, Vera Jones, and Stephen Raw.

Can you find the little bear
in each scene?

P.B. BEAR'S
CHRISTMAS

Lee Davis

DK PUBLISHING, INC.

There were only 2 more days until Christmas!

P.B. Bear  jumped out of  .

He took off his  and put on his  and  .

KNOCK! KNOCK! KNOCK!

Mailman Monkey  was standing at the  .

He had a big  for  . It was a

Christmas surprise from Grandma Bear  !

"Here's something for you," said  .

He gave  a Christmas invitation.

Dear Mailman,
You are invited to my house for Christmas Day.

Love from P.B. Bear

Dear Mailman,
You are invited to
my house for
Christmas Day.
Love f   D.B. Bear

took his Christmas inside. He put on his cosy red , his blue , and his stripy .

"Come and play in the snow!" called Florrie and Dermott . They rolled and patted the .

Can you guess what they were making?

used 1 for a nose, 2 for eyes, and 3 for buttons. found some to make a smile!

"Look!" laughed .

"A snow bear!"

Later,  and  sipped  of hot chocolate,

while  snored loudly.

KNOCK! KNOCK! KNOCK!

 was at the  with more  for  !

"Brrr!"  shivered. "It's cold out here in the snow."

"Come in and warm your feet by the ," said  .

"I'd like to," said , "but I've got more

and  to deliver."

There was only 1 more day until Christmas.

"Let's decorate the 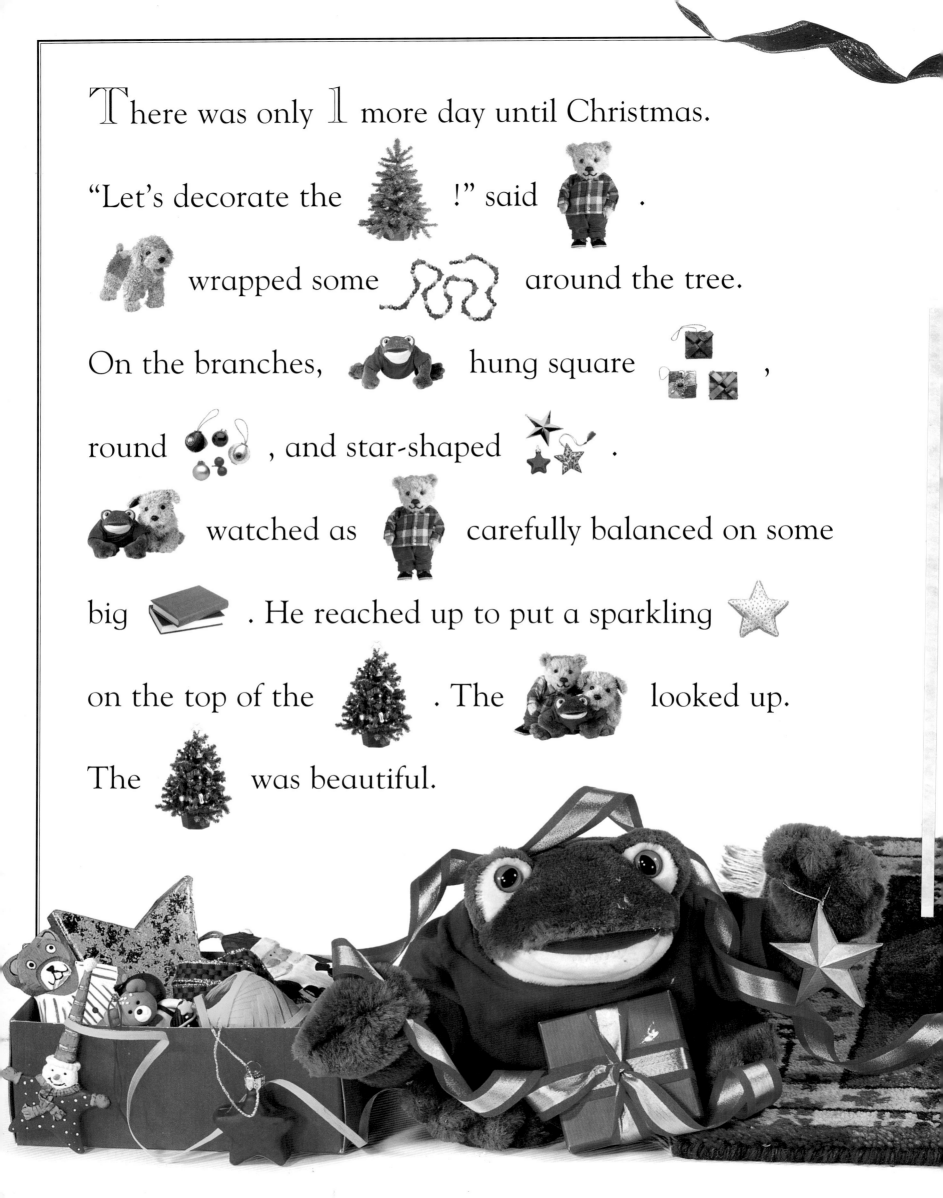 !" said 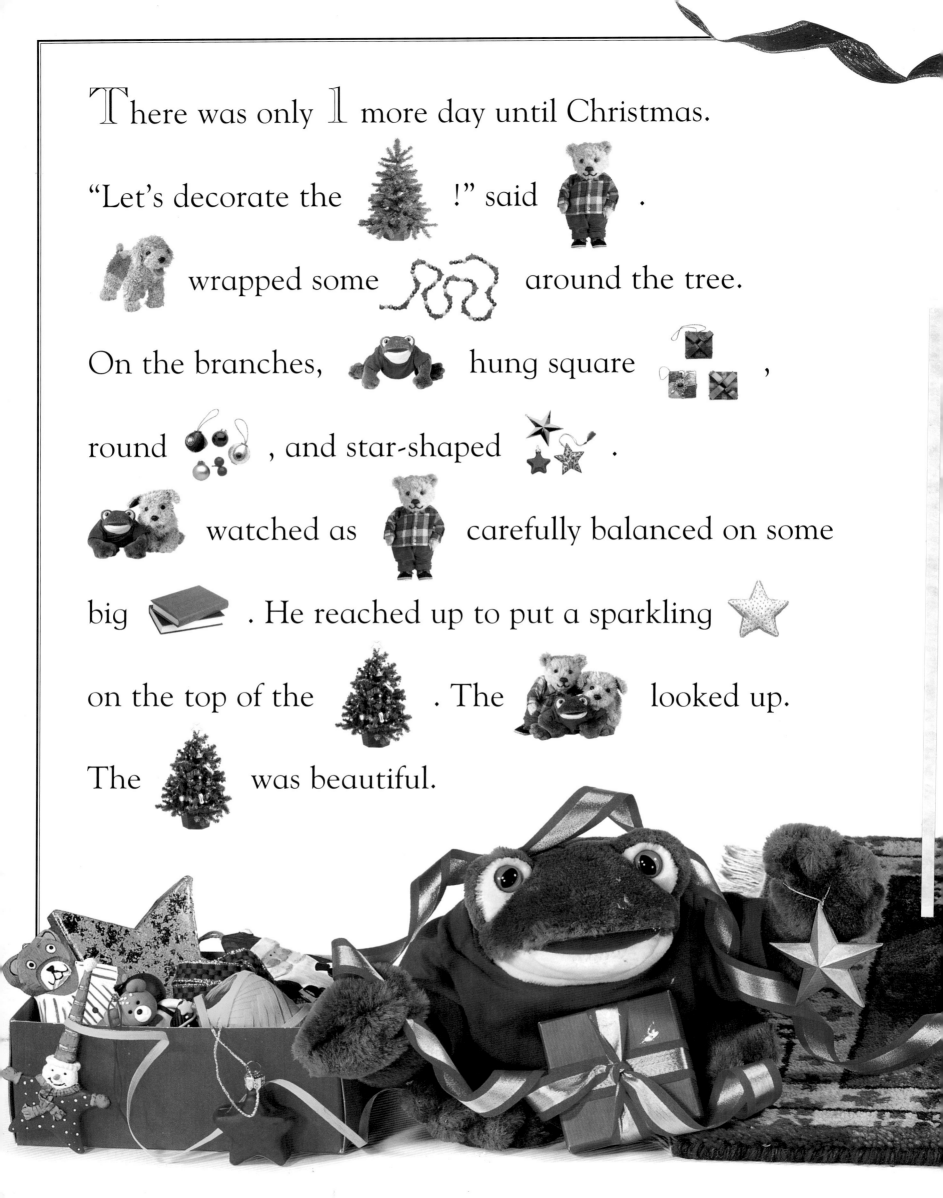 .

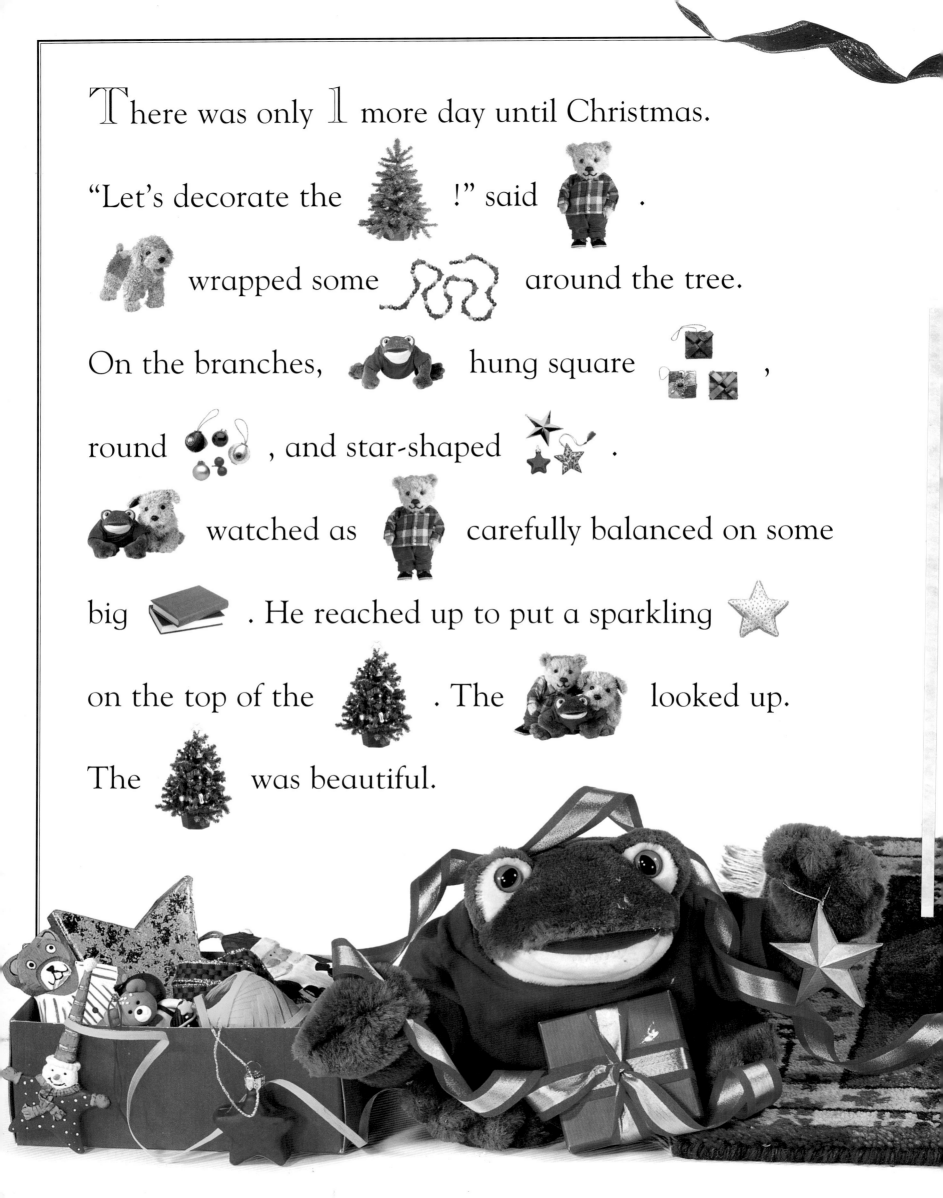 wrapped some around the tree.

On the branches, hung square ,

round , and star-shaped .

 watched as carefully balanced on some

big . He reached up to put a sparkling

on the top of the . The looked up.

The was beautiful.

It was the night before Christmas!

 put on his 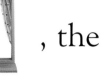 . Now he was ready for  .

Outside his  , the   twinkled in the night sky.

"I wonder how many   there are," thought  .

He began to count, $1, 2, 3$ . . . soon he was fast asleep.

Good night, P.B. Bear . . .  .

That night, dreamed he was riding across the sky with Snow Bear . They waved to the and the . The

pulled the 🛷 low over the 🏘️ pub helped 🧸 deliver his 🎁

It was Christmas Day at last!

"Merry Christmas!" said  to his .

There were lots of for them to open.

"Look at my new !" said .

"And my !" said .

"These will keep me warm!"

laughed .

carefully opened his 🎁 from 🧸 .

Something inside twinkled. What could it be?

"My very own Christmas ✨ !"

P. B. Bear

Franny

Dermott

bed

pajamas

pants

shirt

door

snowballs

snow bear

pebbles

Christmas tree

beads

decorations

reindeer

sleigh

houses

presents

Mailman
Monkey

Grandma
Bear

Snow
Bear

friends

package

invitation

sweater

hat

scarf

twigs

mugs

Christmas
cards

fireplace

packages

books

star

window

stars

moon

presents

bowl

necklace

socks

stars